The Adventures of

Seek and Save

Lost at Sea

Written by Sharon Swanepoel

Illustrated by Lucas Loscinto

Dedicated to the Unborn.

God's Glory Ministries International Inc.

A God's Glory Media Publication

Author: Sharon Swanepoel
P. O. Box 1430
Dacula, GA 30019, USA.
www.GodsGlory.org
E-mail: sharon@godsglory.org

Illustrator: Lucas Loscinto
Website: http://strvnartist.googlepages.com/
E-mail: strvnartist@gmail.com
Tel: 540.710.4486

Layout and design: Rudi Swanepoel

The Adventures of Seek & Save: Lost at Sea
ISBN: **978-0-9772647-2-8**

Thank you to Almighty God for inspiring the dream and creating it in me, for
designing the original concept of seeking and saving the lost.
To Rudi, my wonderful husband, thank you for believing in me to do what I never
ever dreamed possible. Also for all your hard work on the layout and cover design.
You are the best. I love you.
To Lucas for all your work on the illustrations, you are an answer to prayer.
There are many great God-things still in store for you.
To my Dad, thanks for teaching me rhyme at an early age.
"Give a grunt and a squeeze."
To Mom, thanks for praying. I love you both!

Printed and bound in China

Hello. My name is Tell,
 I would love to share with you this story
  from my adventure inventory
  It is of Seek and Save who found a way
   to rescue a family one stormy day.

Seek sat on the deck of Save's rescue boat, this day had started on a lovely note. The ocean was a glistening blue with an aqua hue. The sun was shining and on the horizon Seek saw puffy clouds arising.

The seagulls were crying out from above. It was a sound that Seek just loved. Seek took a sip of his tea and looked across the sea. More than fifty ships he could count. But the yellow one just had to be the nicest one sailing about.

As the yellow vessel sailed by Seek gave an approving sigh.
It was Mr. Scott who captained the yellow yacht.
"I like your yacht Mr. Scott"
"Thank you Seek, her name is the Forget-Me-Not."
"Take care sailing out there; a storm I sense is in the air."
"Oh Seek, the sun is still shining here, how could a storm be drawing near?"

And with that he sailed off into the distance,
singing a song with a sailor's persistence:
"Oh my little yacht the Forget-Me-Not.
How pretty you are like a lemon drop."
He sounded the boat's horn.
And gave no notice to the warning of the storm.
Away sailed the yellow yacht
Forget-Me-Not, captained by Mr. Scott.
Who sailed the ocean with his wife and tiny tot.

After enjoying a hearty meal,
Seek and Save felt the ship
Start to rock and reel.
Outside they heard the rumblings of thunder,
The sound of which made them wonder.

Then Seek to Save did say:
"Hope all the vessels we saw today
Are safe and tucked away
in the harbor of Shelly Bay."

Save was listening to Seek
Sing one of his favorite songs.
While the wind outside produced
an accompaniment of howls and gongs.

Seek's voice at times
sounded loader than thunder.
The song's calming words put all fears
asunder.

Seek was short and stout
But his song was like a shout and without a doubt
Even his moustache was alive and moving about.
The fish on his bib was a speckled trout
Which moved with every note as he pushed his belly out.

He Sang:

Jesus in the boat

If you're going to sail upon the ocean
And you have a funny notion
That a storm is coming your way
Let Jesus into your boat today

Storms may come you can smile at them all
In His care you'll feel cozy and warm
Even if you're soaked and chilled to the bone
You can be warm if your heart is His home

The rains may come and the winds may blow
God's great peace in the storm He will show
Remember His feet walked upon waters deep
You will be safe and sound in His keep

With Jesus in your boat you can smile at the storm
In His presence you'll feel cozy and warm
Even if you're soaked and chilled to the bone
You are warm if your heart is His home

Just as Seek was finishing the last note
Both were alarmed at the thunder outside the boat.
Suddenly inside the radio started to crackle.
Seek was so startled
He almost stepped into Save's fishing tackle.

Somebody was sounding an S.O.S.
That's a call for help when you are in distress.
The Forget-Me-Not was lost on the ocean
A rescue mission was set in motion.

With Save at the helm and Seek at the bow,
Through the stormy waters the boat did plow
The waves were high, reaching up to the sky
And for the yellow yacht they kept a watchful eye

With a "CRACK" and a "SLAP" the waves came crashing down
While the waters churned all around
Save knew his boat would weather the storm
After all they had a rescue to perform.

They broke through the waves from bottom to top
"UP, UP, UP" then "DOWN" they would drop.
This way and that way they would "BOP" and "PLOP"
Their boat almost did a belly flop!

The yellow yacht was lost at sea.
But together they would find out where she could be
The waves were big but Save was brave.
After all they had a vessel to save.

With every lightning bolt illuminating the sky,
Seek would see a FLASH OF YELLOW nearby.
With his trusty binoculars Seek began to see
Flashes of yellow and he shouted with glee

"HOORAY!"

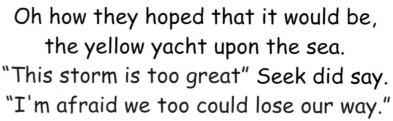

Oh how they hoped that it would be,
the yellow yacht upon the sea.
"This storm is too great" Seek did say.
"I'm afraid we too could lose our way."
Save said: "Seek, aren't you forgetting your song?"
"Let's sing it out loud all night long."

The engine of the boat made a low deep drone,
And the louder the waves and the wind had blown,
They sang the song for they weren't alone,
Singing loud and strong in a bold new tone.

They sang all night long,
and their fears were gone,
as the violent storm raged on and on. . .
Seek and Save's voices were almost gone.
Suddenly in the distance Seek could see
Something was moving. What could it be?

Seek strained his eyes further to gaze.
There it was again bobbing in the haze.
It was Captain Scott in the water,
With his wife and Dot, their daughter.
Captain Scott cried out: "HELP"
His voice they could hear.
Even the cry of his daughter,
Brought them cheer.
Out over the ocean Seek did peer,
As Save threw out the rescue gear.

Seek watched as Save dove in
To rescue the Scotts "let the swimming begin..."
Huge breaking waves he plowed right through.
He cried out: "Don't worry now I'm here to save you"

Save tried to keep the Scotts in view,
The closer he got in courage he grew.
He was strong and oh so brave,
His beard was stubble and he needed a shave.
He would put his life in danger. Even for a stranger.
The current was strong, but it did not take him long,
To reach Mrs. Scott and her daughter, little Dot.
With a rope Save tied a good strong knot.

They held on tight to the rescue float,
As Save attached the heavy rope.
With a "HEAVE" he pulled them right into the boat,
While Seek poured them tea from the flask in his tote.

Mrs. Scott and Dot were now safe and sound,
But Mr. Scott was still out of bounds.
Seek could tell the rescue was going well.
Poor Mrs. Scott so weary, on the deck she fell.

Both she and Dot were safely onboard.
Seek gave thanks to the Lord.
Now it was Mr. Scott's turn,
Save's eyes of the salt began to burn.

If only the waves could settle down,
Mr. Scott was afraid that he would drown.
Suddenly he was swept under a mighty wave,
He feared the seas would become his watery grave.
Seek looked but all he could see,
Was a captain's hat were Mr. Scott used to be!

Breaking the surface he yelled out: "Save, Save. . .!"
While frantically with his hands he waved.
With a cough and a choke he gurgled a cry. . ."Uh!"
With hope he realized fear was a lie,
For just then a rope through the air did fly.
He had to swim closer he just had to try!

A life preserver landed in front of him there.
He tried to reach out and whispered a prayer.
He grabbed hold of it with both of his hands,
While drawing him in Save took a firm stand.

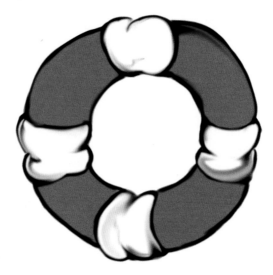

Mr. Scott tried to reach the side of the vessel,
While against the waves he had to wrestle.
Save "HEAVED" and "HEAVED"
With a great "GRUNT" and a "SQUEEZE"
And yelled out "Just hold on tight please!"

Save could not get Mr. Scott into the boat,
So over the side he threw a net made of rope.
Mr. Scott climbed the net just like he would a ladder,
Save coiled up the rope,
Which almost looked like a puff adder.

Mr. Scott now too was safely onboard.
"YIPPEE" they all shouted "Let's give thanks to the Lord!"
With the Scotts now snug and dry,
They headed for the harbor that was nearby.

Still the yellow yacht, Forget-Me-Not, was lost at sea.
Mr. Scott was crying: "Oh, were could she be?"
"We will search for her tomorrow in the light of day"
Seek said: "now we should return to Shelly Bay."

While sailing home they taught the Scotts their favorite song.
The journey to Shelly Bay did not take them long.

Seek and Save were so brave that day,
There they were snoring away "ZZZZZZ"
Mr. Scott lay awake a prayer to pray:
"Lord please let us find my Forget-Me-Not … today"
"S-S-SOB…" He cried crocodile tears,
In prayer he let go of his fears.

In the dark Mr. Scott lay upon his bed
Thinking of the Yellow Yacht. . . "Oh!"
She was so bright and pretty like a lemon drop.
Was she safe and sound or was she on the rocks?
And while he was thinking he twiddled his toes,
Looking at the holes in his socks.

Morning came and they were back on the ocean,
To search for the yellow yacht their noses covered with suntan lotion.
The gulls were even more rowdy than the day before,
A more beautiful day they could not ask for.

Deeper and deeper into the waters they sailed,
Mr. Scott so worried started biting his nails. "YUCK!"
Seek was sure he knew were the yellow yacht could be;
There was a secret cove were Save once fell and hurt his knee.
"OUCH!"
In the distance they could see a yellow sail waving about.
As they entered the cove they had no more doubt.
They had found the yellow yacht!
"HOORAY!" They all shouted out.
Seek said: "Just look Captain Scott it's the Forget-Me-Not!"
He cried: "Oh my pretty lemon drop!"

"Thank you Seek and Save" the Scotts did say,
"In the storm we went astray,
You rescued us and now the Forget-Me-Not today.
Next time your warning we'll obey."
With that they happily sailed away.

Wow did you enjoy that?
Hope Mr. Scott found his hat.
This story of Seek and Save
makes me think of Jesus.
He came to seek and save us
from our ocean of sin.
The Bible says that we all
are lost and dying in sin,
So we need a Savior,
Who will give us life within.

Jesus was once in a storm,
and even walked on water to rescue His friends.
He saved them from a stormy sea.
Even in the midst of the storm,
He could hear their plea.

Did you know that Jesus wants to come into your
life and be your friend too?
You will never be the same, He will make you new.

We all have been lost on the ocean of sin,
Only Jesus can save us and make us new within.
Jesus died on a cross, then
from the dead He rose on day three,
Giving His life because He loves you and me.

Jesus came to seek us out of the storms of life
and save us from the seas of sin.
He came to give us new life and make us win.
Jesus is strong and very brave,
He has already conquered sin's fierce waves.

Just like Mr. Scott, we do not obey God's warnings,
And end up in trouble.
In the storm, without Jesus, your life will turn to rubble.
So call on Jesus and repent of your sin,
He will give you a new life to begin.

When you are in a storm or a scary situation,
Call on Jesus, He will find your location,
He will take you to a peaceful destination,
And give you His salvation.
You do not need to send an S.O.S.
Just pray when you are in distress.

Would you like Jesus to be your Savior?
Pray this prayer, you will be doing yourself a favor.

Dear Jesus
I ask You to come into my heart today.
Come and wash all my guilt and sin away.
Forgive me that in sin I went astray.
Make me Your child this I pray.
Teach me to walk in You, the Way.
All my cares and burdens on You I lay.
Thank You for loving me in every way.
Teach me Your will in all I do and say.
All this in Jesus' Name I pray.
Amen

Jesus Said: "the Son of Man has come
to seek and to save
That which was lost."
Luke 19:10

Memory Verses
Luke 19:10
For the Son of Man has come to seek and to save
that which was lost.

John 3:16
For God so loved the world that He gave His only begotten Son,
that whoever believes in Him should not perish but have
everlasting life.

Acts 2:21
And it shall come to pass That whoever calls on the name of the
LORD Shall be saved.

John 14:14
If you ask anything in My name I will do it.

Jesus walks on a stormy sea
John 6:16-21
Now when evening came, His disciples went down to the sea, got into the boat, and went over the sea toward Capernaum. And it was already dark, and Jesus had not come to them. Then the sea arose because a great wind was blowing. So when they had rowed about three or four miles, they saw Jesus walking on the sea and drawing near the boat; and they were afraid. But He said to them, "It is I; do not be afraid." Then they willingly received Him into the boat, and immediately the boat was at the land where they were going.

BECOME A FISHER OF MEN

Would you like to join Seek and Save
on the mission that Jesus gave
Just like Seek and Save you
can reach out to others too.
Read this scripture and
you will know what to do:

And then he told them,
"Go into all the world and
preach the Good News to
everyone, everywhere.
Mark 16:15

You can rescue your friends just by
telling them about Jesus.
Tell them that He loves us all and
that His love still frees us

So wherever you are and wherever you may go
To seek and save, God's love you must show.
Do not stop at one, but let the whole world know
So the Kingdom of God will begin to grow.

Take on this mission and you will see
And part of Seek and Save's adventure you will be.
Reaching out for your friends to see
Jesus in you; a reality.

So show His love and say a prayer
Jesus will be with you right there.
As you too seek and save the lost
At any cost.

Quiz time with Tell

Questions:

1. What was the name of the yellow yacht?
2. Who rescued Mr. Scott?
3. Who walked on water to save His friends?
4. How many ships did Seek see sailing about?
5. What is an S.O.S.?
6. Who can save you from your sin?
7. What did Seek almost step into?
8. Who was at the helm of the rescue vessel?
9. Who rose on day three?
10. Where did Seek keep a flask of his tea?
11. Who had holes in his socks?
12. What was the name of Mr. Scott's daughter?
13. Why did Mr. Scott lie awake?
14. What was drifting on the water where Mr. Scott used to be?
15. What should you do when you are in a stormy situation?

Answers:

1. The Forget-Me-Not.
2. Save.
3. Jesus.
4. Fifty.
5. It's a call for help when you are in distress.
6. Jesus
7. Save's fishing tackle.
8. Save.
9. Jesus
10. In a tote on the boat.
11. Mr. Scott.
12. Dot.
13. A prayer to pray.
14. A captain's hat.
15. Call on Jesus.

✳ Seek & Save: Lost at Sea CD
A CD of fun songs with Seek & Save

✳ Seek & Save and the Pirates of Praise
A new adventure with Pirates, Treasure hunts,
and our own heroic Seek & Save

✳ Seek & Save: Lost in the Dark
In this new adventure Seek & Save
search for a missing boy in a dark cave.
Will they find him in time?

About the Author

Sharon has a heart for evangelism and travels the world with her husband, Rudi, proclaiming the Gospel of Jesus Christ.

She is a friend of the next generation. Projects like this one was driven by her passion to encourage children to know Jesus, while teaching them the core truths that will equip them for life. Her vision is to place books like this in the hands of children worldwide and thus share with them the Good News of Jesus Christ early in their formative years.

An accomplished musician / composer with several published Cd's, she now steps into a new genre with a prayer for transformed lives all over the world.
For more information visit www.GodsGlory.org

Sharon Swanepoel

About the Illustrator

Lucas Loscinto

Lucas is an artist with a tremendous God-given ability to bring characters to life. Known for his amazing murals, he agreed to apply his gift to this project.

He has a heart for children, a passion for God and an artist's eye for detail.

He resides in Spotsylvania, VA.